HIDDEN

by Nicola Werenowska

Published by Playdead Press 2017

© Nicola Werenowska 2017

Nicola Werenowska has asserted her rights under the Copyright, Design and Patents Act, 1988, to be identified as the authors of this work.

A CIP catalogue record for this book is available from the British Library.

ISBN 978-1-910067-45-1

Caution

All rights whatsoever in this play are strictly reserved and application for performance should be sought through the author before rehearsals begin. No performance may be given unless a license has been obtained.

This book is sold subject to the condition that it shall not by way of trade or otherwise, be lent, resold, hired out, or otherwise circulated without the publisher's prior consent in any form of binding or cover other than that in which it is published and without a similar condition including this condition being imposed on the subsequent purchaser.

Playdead Press
www.playdeadpress.com

HIDDEN

by Nicola Werenowska

Chris   Lewis Goody
Jess   Milli Proust

Director   Scott Hurran
Designer   Loren Elstein
Lighting Designer   Zoe Spurr
Sound Designer   Max Pappenheim
Stage Manager   Kerri Charles
Producer   Maeve O'Neill & Ecclesia Theatre Company

After showings at Graeae and the Mercury Theatre, Hidden premiered at Oxford Playhouse in April 2017 before touring to Norwich Arts Centre, The Marlowe Theatre and the Mercury Theatre.

HIDDEN has been funded by Arts Council England and developed in association with the Mercury Theatre, Graeae Theatre Company and English Touring Theatre Forge.

CAST

Lewis Goody | Chris

Lewis trained at Guildhall School of Music & Drama. Theatre includes: *As You Like It* (Watch Your Head, Windsor Great Park); *Romeo and Juliet* (HomeMCR); *The Winter's Tale* (Regents Park Open Air Theatre); *Top Story* (Old Vic Tunnels). TV includes: *Doctors* (BBC). Film includes: *DJ* (Project London). Lewis also hosts a podcast on iTunes called Acting Inspired, chatting to inspiring actors and documenting events in his career with a view to inspire others. @actinginspired

Milli Proust | Jess

Milli is a graduate from RADA and this year has shot the short film *Salmon*, written and directed by Liam Creighton. Last year, Milli performed in *Vernon God Little* at The Space directed by Katherine Timms and Max O'Brien produced *The Lore of the Land* for Radio 4. Other theatre includes: *It Felt Like A Kiss* (Punchdrunk) and most recently, Milli starred as Cinderella at Windsor Castle (Watch Your Head), and performed a one woman show at Theatre 503.

CREATIVE TEAM

Scott Hurran | Director

Scott trained at the Royal Central School of Speech and Drama and RADA. Film includes: *Career Boy* (Official Selection Raindance Film Festival); *Medicine Man* (Official Selection Cannes Film Festival, Short Film Category). Theatre: Hurran is Artistic Director of Ecclesia. *Counting Stars* by Atiha Sen Gupta (Assembly, Edinburgh Fringe), shortlisted for the Amnesty International Freedom of Expression Award; *The Game* by Sam Freeman (Courting Drama, Southwark Playhouse); *The House of Bernarda Alba* (Kings Head Theatre); *Three to Four Days* (Theatre 503); *Immigrant* (Theatre Uncut, Young Vic); *The Grandfathers* (National Theatre Connections, Theatre Chipping Norton and Oxford Playhouse); and *The Seventh Continent* (Prague Quadrennial). Assistant Directing credits include: *I Call My Brothers* by Jonas Hassen Khemiri, (dir. Tinuke Craig, Gate Theatre); *The Precariat* by Chris Dunkley (dir. Chris New); *Theatre Uncut* (dir. Emma Callander, Theatre Uncut, Young Vic). *This Same England* (dir. Elizabeth Freestone, RSC and Pentabus Theatre).

Loren Elstein | Designer

Loren is an international designer for theatre, opera and film. She trained at NIDA in Sydney where her designs for *Loot* secured her the Australian Production Design Guild Award for Best Design and the William Fletcher Foundation Grant for Excellence in Design 2013. Theatre and film work includes: *The Ugly One* (Park Theatre, Dir. Roy A Weisse); *Rosencrantz and Guildenstern Are Dead* (Associate Set Design, Co-costume Design, The Old Vic); *Rent 20th Anniversary Tour* (Costume Design, Michael Grandage Company, Dir. Bruce Guthrie); *Primetime* (Royal Court Theatre, Dir. Roy A Weisse); *Stoneface* (Finborough Theatre, Dir. Roy A Weisse); *The End of Longing* (Associate Design, Playhouse Theatre, Dir. Lindsay Posner); *Wanderous Strange (RSC Dir. Lina Johnson); A Room of Her Own* with *Mimbre Acrobats* (The Southbank Centre-WOW Festival Dir: Lina Johansson); *The Man Who Almost Killed Himself* (Summer Hall for Edinburgh Festival (BBC iPlayer); *Ten Women* (Oval House); and circus show *Polymer* (Udderbelly Festival,Southbank, Dir. Lina Johansson). Art Direction for *Magic FM*; FatBoy Slim's *The Collection 30"* and Mcbusted's *Most Excellent Adventure Tour* Music Videos. Opera designs include: *A Midsummer*

Night's Dream (Theater Trier, Dir. Sam Brown); *Pia de Tolomei* (English Touring Opera, Dir. James Conway); *The Water Palace* (Tête à Tête Festival, Dir. Sam Brown).

Zoe Spurr | Lighting Designer

Zoe works as a lighting designer and associate both in the UK and worldwide. Zoe graduated from Central School of Speech and Drama. Recent theatre lighting designs include *School Play* with antic | face (Southwark Playhouse); *Good Dog* with Tiata Fahodzi (Watford Palace, UK Tour); *Muted* (Bunker Theatre); *Erwartung/Twice Through The Heart* with Shadwell Opera (Hackney Showroom); *The Knife Of Dawn* (Sackler Studio, Roundhouse); *Affection* and *Hookup*, with Outbox Theatre Company (Hackney Showroom/Contact Manchester/Site Specific) *Torch* and *This Evil Thing* (Edinburgh Fringe Festival 2016); *A Serious Case of The F*ckits* and *The Heresy of Love* (Central); *Bitches* (NYT, Finborough Theatre). Corporate designs include: the *Terry Pratchett Final Book Launch* (Waterstones, Piccadilly Circus); *Grey Goose Fly Beyond* (Welsh Presbyterian Chapel, Shaftesbury Avenue). Associate work includes: *The Trilogy* (The Donmar Warehouse, Kings Cross); *1984* (Playhouse Theatre); *Derren Brown- Infamous, Eric and Little Ern* and *The Only Way is Downton* (touring).

Max Pappenheim | Sound Designer

Theatre includes: *The Children* (Royal Court); *Sex with Strangers*, *Labyrinth* (Hampstead Theatre); *Ophelias Zimmer* (Schaubühne, Berlin and Royal Court); *Sheppey*, *Blue/Heart*, *Little Light*, *The Distance* (Orange Tree Theatre, Richmond); *The Gaul* (Hull Truck); *Toast* (Park Theatre and 59E59 Theatres, New York); *Jane Wenham* (Out of Joint); *Waiting for Godot* (Sheffield Crucible); *My Eyes Went Dark* (Traverse, Edinburgh); *Cargo* (Arcola Theatre); *CommonWealth* (Almeida Theatre); *A Lovely Sunday for Creve Coeur* (Print Room); *Wink* (Theatre503); *Fabric*, *Invincible* (National Tours); *Spamalot*, *The Glass Menagerie*, *Strangers On A Train* (English Theatre, Frankfurt); *Kiki's Delivery Service*, *Johnny Got His Gun*, *Three Sisters*, *Fiji Land*, *Our Ajax* (Southwark Playhouse); *Mrs Lowry and Son* (Trafalgar Studios); *Martine*, *Black Jesus*, *Somersaults*, *The Fear of Breathing* (Finborough Theatre); *The Faction's Rep Season 2015* (New Diorama Theatre); *Shopera: Carmen* (Royal Opera House); *The Hotel Plays* (Langham Hotel). As Associate, *The Island* (Young Vic); *Fleabag* (Soho Theatre). Associate Artist of The Faction. Radio includes *Home Front* (BBC Radio 4).

Kerri Charles | Stage Manager

Kerri graduated from The Royal Welsh College of Music and Drama in 2015 and RADA in 2013. She completed her first professional Stage Management job at the Edinburgh Fringe Festival with a theatre comedy called *Tracy* (2016). She was Company Stage Manager for the UK Tour of *Shakespeare His Wife and the Dog* with Bated Breath Theatre (2016). She was Company Stage Manager for the Little Fish Theatre Company for their London tour of *Seventeen to the Power of 3* (2017). She worked with Grange Park Opera as a member of the lighting team and works as a freelance technician on events such as the Theatre Royal Winchester's annual Hat Fair.

Maeve O'Neill | Producer

Maeve is an independent arts producer, specialising in theatre producing and mentoring. Maeve has produced national tours for poet, Simon Mole, Novus Theatre, NIE Theatre and the first production of Blind Summit's award winning show, *The Table* at Edinburgh 2011. She works on a regular basis with artists, theatre companies and venues including Ovalhouse, Apples and Snakes and Ambreen Razia. She trained at The Gaiety School of Acting, Dublin and completed a BA in Modern Drama Studies at Brunel University.

Nicola Werenowska | Writer

After a brief flirtation with playwriting when she was 16 (her first play "20%" was runner-up in the 1988 Royal Court Young Playwrights' Competition), Nicola began her playwriting journey by joining a local playwrights' group in 2003, following her life transforming diagnosis of dyspraxia. Since then she has established herself as a successful playwright with productions including: *Davy's Day* (Mercury, 2004); *Peapickers* (Eastern Angles, 2007); *Freedoms of the Forest* (Menagerie, 2008); *Birth-Date* (Nabakov, 2012, part of 'Best Years' series); *CASH!* (Mercury, 2013); *Tu I Teraz* (Hampstead, the Nuffield, the Mercury, 2012/13); *Tattooed Under Your Skin* (Theatre 503, Acts of Defiance Festival, 2016). Her work has been shortlisted for national playwriting competitions including the Verity Bargate, and long-listed for the Bruntwood and Papa Tango. Nicola has been a writer on Graeae's attachment scheme, 'Write to Play', a member of the Royal Court National Writers' group and is playwright in residence at Essex University.

AUTHOR'S NOTES

To two strong women who changed my life in an instant and forever:

In Ruth Green, who identified my invisible disability where no one else had, I found someone who finally listened.

Ruth – thank you for discovering the truth of who I am.

In Mary Colley, whose pioneering work with and for dyspraxic adults has been lifesaving for many undiagnosed dyspraxics including myself, I found a role model – someone who dared to follow her passion despite and because of her disability.

Mary – know wherever you are that I kept my promise: that this play is for you.

ACKNOWLEDGEMENT AND THANKS

This production of HIDDEN has been made possible by the generous support of the following organisations:

Grants For The Arts (East), Mercury Theatre, English Touring Theatre Forge, Graeae Theatre, the Dyspraxia Foundation, Dyscovery Centre, Essex Book Festival, Lakeside Theatre, Centre for Cognition, Kinesthetics and Performance at the University of Kent.

Thanks to: Jutta Austin, Amanda Kirby, Ruth Green, Maxine Roper, Nina Finbow, Charles Watson, Mark and Sue Werenowski, Amanda Haberland Jones, Rich Chilver, Marek Rencki, Patsy Humm, Richard and Violet Brice, Helen Bitner, Angela Eyre, Alison Fogg, Nicola Shaughnessy, Daniel Buckroyd, Dan Sherer, Neil Jones, Andrew Burton, Carissa Hope Lynch, Rob Drummer, Anthony Lau.

Special Thanks to: a wonderful cast and creative team.

CHARACTERS

Jess: 23, History Ph.D. student

Chris: 28, aspiring City lawyer

Action takes place between 2005 and 2011.

1.

CHRIS: It is September 2005 and he is 28 years old. The city is booming and life is a whirlwind. And on the tube, he scrutinises the faces of the other suits – and he can tell. Who looks washed out? Who can play the game? Who's going to make it? He can tell because he can read people's faces. And in court it is never what you say but always how you say it. Always a performance and he is a performer. A winner, a fucking winner. He is a winner and today, he won, Harwis versus Jaywood, he won everything. And costs. Costs and everything. (*beat*) And Slime, that's a nickname, Slime, senior partner, who doesn't do compliments, put his hand on his shoulder and said, like he was the Queen or fucking Thatcher, 'We are impressed, Chris.' (*quietly*) He called him by his name. (*beat*) And in that moment, standing on the steps outside Beau Law Courts, he feels the dream of junior partnership... come closer, as if he could reach out and touch it. (*beat*) He can't. (*beat*) Not yet. (*beat*) But they are expanding, new offices by Mansion House, the deal is going through, alliances are being forged by the photocopier, hushed broken chats by the water dispenser and there he is in the thick of it – and he wants it – junior partnership – he wants it like… like he's never wanted anything else. (*beat*) When he was a kid, he wanted to touch the moon. (*beat*) He wouldn't believe it was impossible. (*pause*)

Notting Hill Gate. Sharp turn left, exit two. He races up the stairs, because he is always in a hurry and his mobile is flashing and as the thought is starting to crystallise in his mind, 'Shit!', 'What did I forget?' he reads 'UCL bar 8ish. Clive etc coming. Cheap bar, hot women. Are you up for it?' (*laughing*) Noah. His mate, Noah, still a student, still a kid. And, walking past *Oddbins* into the upmarket wine merchant's next door, looking for something 'special' to celebrate his victory, 'Do you have a *Chablis* with a kick?' he's thinking, why do I need a cheap bar? And appreciating the design on the label, 'Yeah, that will be fine, thanks,' he remembers the giddiness of pint races, chain smoking, coke snorting, girl fumbling and he thinks that was another time, another London. And turning now into his road of gleaming white houses, his road where he is a property owner – it is about location and not square metres – he relishes, as he does most nights, the prospect of an evening in, the calmness of the flat, the gooseberry finish of the wine, hours of endless channel hopping. (*beat*) And then he thinks of the women. (*picks up phone*)

2.

Student party. Chris is drunk, slumped on the floor. At a distance, Jess is crawling, looking for her shoe

CHRIS: It is six hours later and the party is in full fucking swing. (*beat*) It is six hours later... he sees her.

JESS: (*speaking at same time*) She sees him.

CHRIS: (*slowly*) He sees her. (*beat*) He doesn't know whether he's down on the floor because he's about to chuck up or whether the strobe lights are doing his head in, or quite possibly both, but there he is... he sees her.

JESS: (*speaking at same time*) She sees him.

CHRIS: (*moving awkwardly towards Jess*) Are you... alright?

JESS: I'm looking for my shoe.

CHRIS: Ah.

JESS: Have you seen it?

CHRIS: No. Is it red?

JESS: Yeah. Same as this one. Are you...?

CHRIS: (*retching*) Yeah, I've had a few, (*beat*) where did you leave it?

JESS: If I knew that...! Are you...?

CHRIS: (*retching*) Yeah.

CHRIS: And somehow, together, somehow... they are getting up, and the room is spinning and he does not want to be there.

JESS: (*speaking at same time*) She doesn't want to be there.

CHRIS: (*to Jess*) One too many.

JESS: It's so crowded.

CHRIS: (*groaning*) The music!

JESS: You call this music?

CHRIS: What would you call it?

JESS: Sound?

TOGETHER: And they are laughing. (*beat*) They are laughing...

CHRIS: And suddenly.

JESS: (*at same time*) And suddenly.

CHRIS: They are...

JESS: This is...

CHRIS: This is...

JESS: They are...

TOGETHER: Suddenly. (*they touch hands, look at one another. pause*)

JESS: Suddenly they are in a cab and she's thinking he's not my type...

CHRIS: (*at same time*) She's not my type.

JESS ...but he offered and it's in the same direction and how else is she going to get home because her mates have gone on somewhere and she hates clubbing.

CHRIS: (*speaking over her*) He hates clubbing.

JESS: And...

CHRIS: And...

TOGETHER: ...and they have something in common.

CHRIS: The noise drives me insane.

JESS: I can't dance.

CHRIS: Yeah, I know the feeling.

JESS: No, I really can't dance. I mean big time really. Like I can't do steps. I mean join them up.

CHRIS: Yeah, I know.

JESS: No, no... you don't. (*beat*) You don't. (*beat*) And in the back of the cab, whistling down Oxford Street with his hands on her knee, she's telling him about failing her bronze ballroom dancing medal. She's telling him how she practised twice a day, how she liked to feel the rainbow sequins on her dress, how she was the only girl in her class, the only girl in Miss Talbot's junior dance academy to fail... (*beat*) and he's laughing, and it *is* funny and she's laughing too, (*beat*) but she hasn't told anyone this before. (*beat*) And she says, 'Have you failed at anything ever?', and he says...

CHRIS: 'No.'

JESS: And he doesn't think about it, but she thinks, what is that like? Not to have failed at anything ever? And she looks at him. And he says...

CHRIS: I'm sorry about your shoe.

JESS: And she says, 'Which one?' And he is laughing, and she says again, 'Which one? I mean this one that's visible or the lost one that's invisible.' And they are laughing together, and they are touching, and kissing, laughing and touching and kissing, and he says...

CHRIS: (*to Jess*) You remind me of my brother.

JESS:	Is that a compliment?
CHRIS:	He loses things all the time.
JESS:	Does he loose shoes?
CHRIS:	Not red ones. Not with heels. Well, not that I know about.
JESS:	They were fifty quid!
CHRIS:	I'll buy you some more.
JESS:	Are you loaded?
CHRIS:	I'm not a student.
JESS:	Are you loaded?
CHRIS:	I work in the city.
JESS:	Is it fun?
CHRIS:	Tough. It's seriously tough. (*beat*) I love it. (*beat*) I lived in Oxfam when I was a student.
JESS:	My Dad got these for me.
CHRIS:	Does he spoil you?
JESS:	He buys me things. (*beat*) He doesn't live with us.
CHRIS:	Snap!
JESS:	Your parents…
CHRIS:	…been divorced for years.
JESS:	I'm sorry.

CHRIS: No, it's fine. (*beat*) And he doesn't tell her about his mum's boyfriends and that he can't remember if they were there before the divorce but certainly after, and coming and going so quickly he couldn't keep up and that when he visits her now, at Easter or Christmas, his mum, long tired of unsuitable boyfriends and focused on Pilates, looks so much smaller that (*slowly*) every time he is taken by surprise.

JESS: And she doesn't tell him about her brother, Clive, in his wheelchair and her mum who's his carer and how she hid in her room for Dad's visits because he only wanted to take *her* out and not Clive, because he said that *she* needed some attention. She doesn't tell him, she can't explain, that it wasn't that she was the favourite – it was that for Dad – Clive didn't exist. (*to Chris*) It's fine. (*they kiss. to self*) But there is something, something they can't quite touch, something they understand, and later, later they will tell each other everything.

CHRIS: (*speaking over her*) Most things.

TOGETHER: Stories.

CHRIS: Later. (*beat*) But now the cab is rolling up at Clanricarde Gardens... (*to Jess*) My road!

JESS: Wow!

CHRIS: (*to Jess*) Do you want to... er...?

JESS: No.

CHRIS: Yeah. I... yeah, (*handing Jess a twenty pound note*), here that should cover you to the Bush.

JESS: Are you...?

CHRIS: Yeah. (*beat*) How about the shoes?

JESS: How about them?

CHRIS: I'd like to buy you a new pair.

JESS: Would you help me choose them?

CHRIS: Fashion's not my thing.

JESS: I'll buy you a latte.

CHRIS: Iced vanilla grande?

JESS: Any way you want.

CHRIS: Tomorrow?

JESS: Tomorrow

TOGETHER: They have a date.

3.

JESS: They have a date. And another and another and it's December 2005 and she's skipping up the stairs to the readers' room in the British Library,

CHRIS: ...And he is running up the steps of the Law Courts,

TOGETHER: ...and meeting on a Friday after work for a pint in Holburn, they are thinking,

CHRIS: Was there ever anyone else?

JESS: Was there before?

CHRIS: What was before? (*pause. to Jess*) I am not a workaholic!

JESS: (*stealing his pint glass*) An alcoholic?

CHRIS: It's Friday night. (*trying to retrieve glass*) Stop it!

JESS: This Saturday, last Saturday, the Saturday before.

CHRIS: Yeah, it's a big case.

JESS: It's always a big case.

CHRIS: Alright, alright, I am work focused. I have to be. (*she returns his drink*)

JESS: A workaholic!

CHRIS: I resent the term. (*beat*) But yeah, it's been full on since law school.

JESS: Me too. I mean the thesis.

CHRIS: What for a whole three months? I'm talking a decade here.

JESS: Seven years is not a decade.

CHRIS: I was estimating.

JESS: But you know, I worked just as hard before. I mean for my undergrad.

CHRIS: (*drinking*) To the conscientious student!

JESS: Just because you messed around at uni!

CHRIS: It was a breeze.

JESS: But you didn't get a first.

CHRIS: Is this where I compliment your brilliant mind and sympathise with any social sacrifices made?

JESS: No, actually I had a good time. (*beat*) I went back for Clive at weekends. (*beat*) Not every weekend. (*beat*) Most of them. It was for mum really, to give her a break.

CHRIS: You don't go back now?

JESS: I do.

CHRIS: Yeah? I thought you spend weekends in bed with me?

JESS: You must be fantasising in the office.

CHRIS: (*laughing*) I'm back by twelve for...

JESS: (*interrupts*) Football...

CHRIS: When I have a match. (*beat*) I'm back for you.

JESS: I should go home more. The thing is now I'm in London it's further...

CHRIS: (*interrupts*) Fifty five minutes...?

JESS: And so expensive.

CHRIS: You've got a young person's...

JESS: (*interrupts*) And now Mum gets respite care at weekends. And... and I like hanging out with you. (*they kiss*)

CHRIS: Do you want another pint?

JESS: No.

CHRIS: Half?

JESS: No.

CHRIS: So...?

JESS: (*interrupts*) There's a new French film...

CHRIS: (*interrupts*) Noah's got a party going.

JESS: We can see it at The Gate.

CHRIS: You don't want to stay in town?

JESS: I don't mind.

CHRIS: Really?

JESS: Really.

CHRIS: Do you want to move in? (*to self. beat*) And he has said it and it is true, but he didn't mean to say it. Not now, not yet, not here. But it's Friday, he's mildly pissed, it's been a fucking good week at work – cases settled, cases won, compliments paid, (*beat*) and he has said it. (*beat*) Sometimes in the week, hitting the calm of the flat, not every night, but sometimes, some nights, he feels not lonely, but... alone and not wanting to be and wanting her. (*beat*) And he's said it. And she says...

JESS: (*to Chris*) Yes. (*beat, to self*) Because... because... because she feels that *this* is the best thing for her. (*to Chris*) I think I'd like another drink.

CHRIS: Champagne?

JESS: Pinot's fine. (*beat*) And while he is perusing the list, she says, (*to Chris* What about my thesis?

CHRIS: (*reading wine list*) You'll be closer to college.

JESS: It takes up so much space.

CHRIS: Isn't it all online?

JESS: Obviously, yeah, but you know, I mean books and files and folders.

CHRIS: We'll squeeze it in. Storage solutions! (*to barman*) Can we get the Merlot?

JESS: I wish I could leave it behind.

CHRIS: What?

JESS: I'm...

CHRIS: What?

JESS: Struggling.

CHRIS: Everyone struggles. No wonder!

JESS: Yeah.

CHRIS: Jess, forget the fucking thesis. It's Friday. To us!

TOGETHER: To us! (*they drink*)

JESS: And she doesn't tell him that she feels out of control that it's a mess that she's a mess that she keeps losing things that she forgets

	to listen in the research seminars that she can't turn the wheels on the filing cabinets at the Institute. She doesn't tell him because... (*beat*)
CHRIS:	Because this is a happy moment.
TOGETHER:	And they are drinking to being young in the city, to the London they love, to what the future holds, to the promise of success, to staying alive, to surviving in a world where you don't know who you are or what you want or what you're hiding.
CHRIS:	And finishing the champagne, they are running,
JESS:	...stumbling...
CHRIS:	...hand in hand towards the tube, lazily searching for a cab to be hailed,
TOGETHER:	...they are going home.

4.

CHRIS: It is April 2006. The months are rolling by and they are working hard.

JESS: Too hard.

CHRIS: They are working hard and they are playing hard. They are seeing the world. Paris, Milan, Warsaw, Budapest, they are serial weekenders and he has a rise and plays golf with Slime, that's a senior partner, on Bank Holidays, and they tick off European cities and (*quietly*) in every city they lose themselves and...

JESS: ...and find each other. (*beat*) And every time she returns to the flat and washes the jet lag out of her hair, she feels her stomach lurch. (*beat*) On Mondays, he shuts the door,

CHRIS: ...exhilarated at the prospect of a new week...

JESS: ...and she sits in front of the screen and some days she feels like crying and other days she doesn't know what she feels and some days her fingers dance wildly over the keyboard as if she is in some small way

	inspired and on other days her hands are dead weights curled around her cup of instant coffee. (*beat*) But every day time is slow. (*pause*)And when he returns, he's patient and kind and cooks her *Tagliatelle* with squid and cherry tomatoes and it's always *al dente*, and he tidies up the flat and organises her thesis into neat piles,
CHRIS:	'Clean desk, clean mind'
JESS:	And at nights he never complains when she wakes up three times sweating (*beat*) but he's not listening. (*beat*) No one's listening.
CHRIS:	(*kissing Jess and opening a bottle of wine*) That is brilliant news.
JESS:	It's just the first year review.
CHRIS:	No, no, no. You have busted your guts and you deserve it.
JESS:	Yeah.
CHRIS:	Come on, you should be... get this down you. (*Jess refuses wine*) Jess? What is it?
JESS:	I don't know.
CHRIS:	You're tired.

JESS: Of course I'm tired. I've been working all night.

CHRIS: Yeah I did notice.

JESS: What does that mean?

CHRIS: Nothing.

JESS: No, no... what are you saying?

CHRIS: I'm saying, yes, you're shattered. Like me after court.

JESS: After court you're like a kite.

CHRIS: And the next day I crash.

JESS: (*angry*) It's not that.

CHRIS: No. (*beat*) I leave my work at the office.

JESS: I work here.

CHRIS: That's not the point. (*beat*) My job is stressful. I deal with it.

JESS: I can't, ok. I can't. (*beat*) Fuck you! Fuck, fuck, fuck you!

CHRIS: Jess, I'm... I'm sorry. I... I got a bollocking from Fuckwit today. It wasn't even my fault, I...

JESS: (*interrupts*) I've got to stop it.

CHRIS: What?

JESS: The thesis.

CHRIS: Are you?

JESS: Yes.

CHRIS: Look, we've been here before…

JESS: (*interrupts*) This time it's different.

CHRIS: You're tired…

JESS: Stop saying that!

CHRIS: I'm trying to be helpful. If you get some sleep…

JESS: (*interrupts*) I can't sleep.

CHRIS: We're going round in circles here.

JESS: I don't want to do it.

CHRIS: Alright.

JESS: And she's telling him. (*Jess mimes words soundlessly or speaks in nonsense language for one minute*) She's telling him and he's listening.

CHRIS: He doesn't understand. (*to Jess*) Look, if you feel so… unhappy, then give it up.

JESS: Really?

CHRIS: You don't need my permission. You've stuck it out, passed your first year, you've had enough. So fucking what? It's not worth ruining your life over.

JESS: Yeah. (*beat*) Yeah. (*beat*) What will I do?

CHRIS: You don't need to decide now. Mull it over. Get some advice. (*beat*) I wouldn't recommend law, or cooking, or waitressing or...

JESS: (*interrupts*) You think I can't do anything?

CHRIS: Hello, I'm joking!

JESS: You're right. I can't do things.

CHRIS: What things?

JESS: I don't know. Stuff. Like other people.

CHRIS: Bollocks!

JESS: I mean like simple things.

CHRIS: Like what?

JESS: I don't know.

CHRIS: I need examples.

JESS: Ok, ok... I can't sew, you know, like sewing on buttons and stuff.

CHRIS: (*laughing*) That is... that's... ridiculous.

JESS: I can't do it.

CHRIS: So what? Who can? I can't sew. This is the twenty first century. Unless you want to be a designer and make...

JESS: (*interrupts*) You mended my jacket.

CHRIS: I took it to the drycleaners.

JESS: No, you said you mended it.

CHRIS: No, I said I fixed it. I facilitated the mending process. Does it matter? Christ, you are giving up your Ph.D. and we're arguing over a fucking button. (*beat*) You'll find something. (*beat*) And while you're getting your head sorted, you can chill out here.

JESS: (*slowly*) How will I live?

CHRIS: I'll help you out. You think I'd let you starve? (*beat*) I could give you an allowance if you wanted.

JESS: (*interrupts*) I'm not a kid.

CHRIS: Everyone needs money. If you stay here, you'll get nothing benefit wise, you'll...

JESS: (*interrupts*) If I stay here. (*pause*)

CHRIS: And he is offering her everything, his flat, his money, his food, he is offering her – this woman – everything, because... because he cannot imagine here without her. Because she is here and now and he wants to tell her she is intelligent and pretty and funny and

	creative and original and of course she will find a job and (*looks at Jess as if trying to speak to her*) …and she's not listening.
JESS:	And in that moment she tries to imagine a world without her thesis, a world without him, but as she clutches at an image, already the shutters are down.
CHRIS:	(*to Jess*) We'll sort it out.
JESS:	Yeah.

5.

JESS: It's July 2006 and now an accomplished job seeker, on the 328 bus to West Hampstead where she has an interview at a primary school, she's suddenly craving cheese and onion crisps with ketchup and as the bus stalls in Maida Vale, her stomach... she... she's... she needs to get off the bus. 'Excuse me, please.' (*beat, she is panting and retching, now off bus*) And slowly recovering and still dreaming of crisps, cheese and onion only, any other flavour makes her retch again, she walks into the nearest Boots and... and walks out again. (*beat*) She doesn't need another test. (*beat*) She needs to tell him. (*whispering to Chris who is working at desk, not listening*) I'm pregnant.

CHRIS: It has been a long day. They are in new premises and the race is on. And even the ergonomic leather chairs do nothing to reduce the tension gripping his lower vertebrae and he is in the middle of drafting a witness statement and it is the middle of

	the afternoon and it is a tricky job and… and she turns up. (*beat*) She is standing there by his desk, not even as much as a text and he thinks, yeah she's fucked up another interview but why does she keep applying for positions that's she's seriously overqualified for? A classroom assistant! Jesus Christ! (*beat*) And trying to keep it under control – all day he has been trying to keep it under control, he looks at her…
JESS:	(*speaking over him*) …she looks away.
CHRIS:	He looks at her and she looks so… so… here… here, she looks so out of place, (*beat*) he is laughing. He cannot stop laughing.
JESS:	What is it?
CHRIS:	Nothing, nothing. (*kisses her*) And she tastes of cheese and onion crisps and her hair is dishevelled and her make up is untidy and he is laughing. And she says,
JESS:	I'm pregnant.
CHRIS:	And the world stops. (*pause*)
JESS:	Say something!

CHRIS: And he thinks if you could rewind time, if you could go back, and he wants her out of the office and the fine details of his witness statement feel suddenly compelling and in need of his tender attention. And he thinks this office will never be the same again and why was he laughing? And will he ever laugh again? And painfully conscious of the unwritten rule 'you never leave the office for personal reasons', he says, (*to Jess*) Do you fancy a coffee?

JESS: A milkshake.

CHRIS: You don't drink milk.

JESS: Banana.

CHRIS: And in the Starbucks next door, while she slurps her milkshake as if she has a lactose addiction, he is dreaming up excuses for his unexpected exit which he's sure will not have gone unobserved, and leaving his *espresso* untouched, he says, (*to Jess*) Are you...?

JESS: Yes.

CHRIS: You've done a test...?

JESS: Two.

CHRIS: And they were...

JESS: Positive. Both of them.

CHRIS: Shit! (beat) Look, you're on the pill. It's supposed to be reliable, right. (*beat*) We should get a refund. I'll sue the pants off them, fucking pharmaceutical morons. Do they...

JESS: (*interrupts*) I forgot...

CHRIS: Forgot...?

JESS: ...to take it.

CHRIS: (*beat*) No. No. You take it every day. I see you take it every day.

JESS: That migraine.

CHRIS: What migraine? Do you want a paracetamol?

JESS: No. Two months ago. When I stayed in bed.

CHRIS: For two days. (*to self*) He forgot her pill.

JESS: (*speaking over him*) She forgot her pill.

CHRIS: (*to Jess*) Look, it's no one's fault.

JESS: Fault? (*beat*) You're talking as if it's a... a bad thing. (*beat*) Is that how you see it?

CHRIS: And he wants to tell her that he doesn't see anything, that everything is blurred, that you think your life is going in one direction, that you're on a path and... (*to Jess*) No, no. Not bad. Not good. I'm shocked. I'm... Jesus!

JESS: Me too.

CHRIS: So... What do you want to do?

JESS: It's a baby.

CHRIS: No, no there is no baby.

JESS: What?

CHRIS: There is a ball of cells attached to the lining of your uterus, that is all there is. Let's not get ahead of ourselves.

JESS: Fuck you!

CHRIS: Jess.

JESS: Fuck, fuck, fuck you!

CHRIS: I'm just saying that... that there are options.

JESS: There are no options. (*to self*) And she's stressed and scared and confused but somewhere, somewhere inside she's excited.

	How could she possibly not be excited? How could anyone...?
CHRIS:	(*interrupts*) What does that mean?
JESS:	You don't have to stay with me.
CHRIS:	(*upset*) Don't. Jess. Don't.

6.

CHRIS: When she tells him, the world stops. (*beat*) But life returns to... Things stay the same but altered.

JESS: Altered but the same.

CHRIS: And time races on. It is March, 2007.

JESS: And the pounds pile on. And she doesn't have to look for a job anymore. Later, when the baby's born, later she'll worry about a job, but now... Now she's waiting, and... waiting and...

CHRIS: And there is the office and he is still hungry, no hungrier, he is the hungriest he has ever been because soon... soon he will have another mouth to feed, (*beat*) and he wants the moon, (*beat*) and working late at night, turning the impossible into the possible he wants the moon so badly he is aching and... (*his mobile rings*)

JESS: I think it's started.

CHRIS: Fuck, are you... have you called an ambulance?

JESS: No, they're only every ten minutes.

CHRIS: You don't want to take any chances. (*to self.*) And urging the cabbie to drive through the red lights to St Marys, 'This is a fucking emergency!' and wondering if he'll make the trial debriefing at eight in the morning, he is thinking, everything will be different and irreversible. Everything is always different and irreversible.

(*Chris enters hospital birthing room, sees Jess*)

JESS: I can't do it.
CHRIS: Are you ok?
JESS: Four centimetres.
CHRIS: Yeah? Wow!
JESS: This is it.
CHRIS: Yeah. (*beat*) Do you want to…?
JESS: I want to stand.
CHRIS: Alright.
JESS: I can't do it.
CHRIS: Do what?
JESS: This. (*picks up gas and air equipment*)
CHRIS: It's easy. You just breathe.

JESS: I can't. I can't breathe.

CHRIS: Like this. Watch. (*he shows her, Jess practises, gets frustrated, he shows her again, she manages to do it and breathes*) (*to self*) And the night is long and the meptid makes her sick and the contractions stop and start and stop and start and stop and stop and… and suddenly there is an oxytocin drip and there are people in the room with different colour coats and he is irrelevant and he doesn't look at their faces and… and there is a baby and it's a boy and breathing and screaming and it is 11am and it is not that he's forgotten to text his absence for the trial debriefing, it's that he chose not to.

7.

JESS: It's July 2007 and most of the time she's the happiest woman on the planet and in the day the baby sleeps peacefully and she naps on the sofa and watches daytime TV without a trace of guilt and eats chocolate biscuits shamelessly – she needs the calories. (*beat*) And one day looking for emergency muslins, she comes across quite by accident her thesis in a box and thinks why didn't she burn it? (*beat*) And that she is another person now. (*beat*) Most days she is the happiest woman on the planet, but sometimes the baby cries and cries and cries and already sleep deprived from night time feeding, she tells herself that babies cry because they are babies and it is natural and that's what they do, but she feels... she... she's pushing the pram faster and faster and faster and nothing's working and she knows now is the time to get out of the flat before... before... she doesn't want to think about it. (*beat*)And she tells herself that everyone finds baby crying wearing and she has a brand new buggy now he's three months and it's lightweight and will be so much easier to negotiate the stairs with and she'll take him to the park and in the fresh air he'll sleep or watch the trees quietly and the crying will stop.

(Jess attempts to fasten the baby in the buggy)

She can't fasten the strap. He is in the buggy and screaming but she can't fasten the strap. She can't do it. 'Stop screaming' she's telling him, 'Shut up!' but she knows it's her, not him, and even if he was fast asleep, it would make no difference. She cannot strap the buggy and she cannot take him out not strapped in. She picks him up, still screaming, and puts him back in the cot. Where are the instructions? She cannot find the instructions and when she eventually does, the diagram is incomprehensible and she cannot fucking do it. (*beat*) She calls him.

CHRIS: And he is about to go into court. (*answering mobile*) Jess?

JESS: Come back.

CHRIS: What?

JESS: Come back.

CHRIS: What's happened? Is he ok?

JESS: I need you.

CHRIS: Is he ok? What's happened?

JESS: Come back now. (*hangs up*)

CHRIS: Jess... Jess. For fuck's sake. (*beat*) And wondering if she used the word emergency or he heard it in her voice, he makes his excuses to Slime, senior partner, 'Domestic emergency, I'm afraid', and Slime, seemingly non-phased, looks at him from beneath his glasses and says 'I'm sure we can manage without you, if it's an emergency.' He says it's ok but his tone is dismissive and of course it is not ok, this is a big trial and he has a big part to play, and he is going home.

CHRIS: (*entering flat*) Jess?

JESS: The straps.

CHRIS: What?

JESS: The buggy, the straps.

CHRIS: Where is he?

JESS: Asleep.

CHRIS: (*walking over to Henry*) Well, that's something.

JESS: I can look after him.

CHRIS: What?

JESS: (*loudly*) I can.

CHRIS: Alright!

JESS: No, no, it's not alright.

CHRIS: No.

JESS: I broke my nails.

CHRIS: You almost broke the bloody buggy by the look of it.

JESS: I'm sorry. (*beat*) The straps. I can't do the straps.

CHRIS: You called me out of work because you couldn't do the straps on the buggy?

JESS: I panicked.

CHRIS: You panicked. Jesus! I was in court. You knew I was in court.

JESS: I forgot.

CHRIS: Yeah. (*beat*) I thought it was an emergency. I'm with a client, and Slime, and we're about to go in. Thank God Counsel was ok about it. (*beat*) Do you know what was going through my head? Do you? (*beat*) Don't call me again like that! I'm in court and you can't work the buggy. Do you know the shit I'm going to face this afternoon? Do you know that the junior partnership will be decided next month or have you forgotten that as well?

JESS: He was crying...

CHRIS: He's a baby.

JESS: and I... I needed to get out.

CHRIS: Why the fuck didn't you?

JESS: Why...?

CHRIS: You could have carried him, you could have put him in the pram, you could have...

JESS: (*interrupts*) Will you show me again?

CHRIS: (*shows Jess how to do buggy*) Fasten, unfasten, fasten, unfasten, fasten, unfasten. Got it?

(*Jess attempts to unfasten straps.*)

CHRIS: Stop! Look, this is… a waste of time!
JESS: Sometimes I think I can't look after him.
CHRIS: No, I didn't say that.
JESS: (*overlapping*) I can't do it.
CHRIS: You can't do the buggy, that's all. (*beat*) Look, let's not get worked up over a rubbish piece of plastic shit knocked up in some sweat shop in China. On Saturday we'll go down to John Lewis and find a buggy that you can do. There are millions of the bloody things. You can try them out, and I'll be patient and fuck the expense.
JESS: It's not about the buggy.
CHRIS: If you had one that was more… user-friendly… you wouldn't have a nervous breakdown every time you want to take him out of the house and I wouldn't get

	bollocked for running out of the office and put my career in jeopardy.
JESS:	Your career...? (*beat*) Shit! have I... the partnership?
CHRIS:	It's alright.
JESS:	Really?
CHRIS:	I am in there. (*beat*) I told them it was an emergency, they understand.
JESS:	I didn't want to call you. I mean...
CHRIS:	Your timing was shit.
JESS:	My timing's always shit.
CHRIS:	Yeah. (*they laugh*)
JESS:	I'm sorry.
CHRIS:	It's alright. (*beat*) Come on, it's alright. (*beat*) And suddenly he is fishing for the box in his pocket. He bought it two weeks ago – their first family outing, Kensington Palace Gardens. It was baking hot and walking past the kids' playground, he'd tried to imagine pushing Henry on a swing and couldn't, but he felt happy to be trying... with the possibility. (*beat*) He'd left her breastfeeding by the pond while he'd

	sneaked off to a jewellers in Kensington Church Street. (*beat*) He puts the box on the table.
JESS:	She looks at it.
CHRIS:	He looks at her. (*beat*) He had been waiting for the partnership to be announced, present her with a double whammy, matching one celebration with another, but this is here and now and he wants to say it, he wants to do it, he wants to move forward with their lives.
JESS:	(*opening box*) She looks at him. And inside there's warmth and laughter and bubbles and… safety. (*beat*) She'll be ok now. He has a job, a career, and they have a baby and it'll all be ok. And she thinks why did I get so upset over a bloody buggy? (*beat*) And she says, (*to Chris*) 'yes'.
CHRIS:	(*breathes sigh of relief*)
JESS:	Yes. Yes, yes, yes. (*they kiss, as if they are about to sex, baby cries, they look at one another, ignore baby.*)

8.

JESS: It's October 2007 and time is ticking and he's late but the gardens are beautiful and Henry's asleep in his user friendly stroller and she feels the warmth of the late afternoon sun on her back and she thinks the anti-depressants must have kicked in because she's enjoying herself and it's not a bad thing to have postnatal anxiety because it's common and the postnatal counsellor said Henry was a shock but she's coping and now with the medication she's coping even better. And (*looking at ring*) there's the wedding and she's planning: lists and lists and lists and they're numbered and she has a special book. It's not until next spring but she is getting ahead. Henry will be one and can stay with her mum – she has it all planned and every time she ticks off a number on her list, she feels... a sense of achievement. (*beat*) But he's still not here. He said by 5 and it's after 6 and the sun is setting and she's suddenly chilly. She doesn't really mind, it was only a walk in the park because he could finish early for once, but she wonders why he hasn't texted, and the park's emptying out and... she sees him. (*calling out*) Chris! (*beat*) But he's not waving and not running towards her but slowly and... stumbling... (*Chris stops at a slight distance to her*) Chris, are you ok?

CHRIS: Yeah.
JESS: You're drunk?
CHRIS: Don't be stupid! Where is he?
JESS: Asleep. Don't wake him!
CHRIS: I won't.
JESS: And don't pick him up when you're drunk.
CHRIS: I'm not fucking drunk.
JESS: Ok, ok.
CHRIS: I had a few pints alright.
JESS: With Noah?
CHRIS: What have you got against him?
JESS: Nothing, (*beat*) he drinks a lot and when you go out with him, you drink a lot too.
CHRIS: So what?

JESS: We had an arrangement.

CHRIS: An arrangement! What are you a business woman now?

JESS: I…

CHRIS: (*speaking over her*) You and your bloody lists and plans. Number One, Number Two… Sometimes, occasionally, I like to be spontaneous. Sometimes I don't want to plan every last detail of every fucking thing.

JESS: Well, I have to plan.

CHRIS: You're neurotic.

JESS: And you're pissed.

CHRIS: I had a hard day, alright.

JESS: Me too. He cried for two hours and…

CHRIS: (*interrupts*) Stop it, alright! Shut the fuck up for one minute! I've been working.

JESS: And what do you think I've been doing?

CHRIS: I don't fucking know.

JESS: Don't drop him! Give him to me.

CHRIS: He's my son.

JESS: Give him to me. (*takes Henry. pause*)

CHRIS: I didn't get the partnership. (*beat*) I said I didn't get the partnership. (*pause*) He has said it aloud. Not for the first time aloud but in the pub with a beer in his hand and the Jukebox playing *Coldplay*, it had seemed… unreal and impossible… and now it is real and she looks at him, blankly.

JESS: She doesn't know what to say

CHRIS: He wants her to say something.

JESS: She doesn't know what to say. Because…

CHRIS: Because nothing she can say will make any difference. Because there are no words. (*beat*) He wanted the moon. (*to Jess*) Say something.

JESS: She wants to say something. She wants to tell him that it's alright because he still has a job, a job that's well paid and challenging and impressive, and there will be other opportunities and maybe… with Henry, maybe the extra stress wouldn't be the best thing right now. She wants to tell him that you can't control everything.

CHRIS: I didn't get it. (*beat*) He wants her to say that... the impossible... you can... the moon... the impossible... he wants. (*to Jess*) I didn't get it.

JESS: I'm sorry.

CHRIS: Yeah.

JESS: But your job, it's ok?

CHRIS: Of course my job is ok, that's not the fucking point.

JESS: I know, I just, I...

CHRIS: (*interrupts*) It's not the job, not the money, it's what I can do. (*beat*) What I want. (*beat*) And he wants to tell her about the moon. (*beat*) She won't understand. (*beat. To Jess*) I've never failed at anything before.

9.

JESS: It's May 2008 and they are on honeymoon in Marrakech and from the top of *Café France*, drinking green tea…

CHRIS: (*to Jess*) Tastes like piss!

JESS: (*to Chris*) You need more sugar.

CHRIS: They are looking down on the snake charmers in the *Jemaa el-Fnaa*, and replaying the wedding in their heads.

JESS: Wow!

CHRIS: Fan-fucking-tastic.

JESS: She's thinking of Clive. The roses around his wheelchair, and how she loved it when he whooped in the ceremony and how Clive's mum tutted, and how her mates from uni came and nobody mentioned her thesis, although they all groaned about their own.

CHRIS: He is thinking of Slime and Fuckwit, hideously paralytic, thumping him on the back at the reception, 'Well done, young man' as if… as if he was almost one of them. (*beat*) The moon is in sight. He is married now, like them. He is respectable, serious... he thinks they get that. He thinks things are on course. It has been a hard year but he is a fighter and he is working harder than ever because there will be another junior partner taken on soon and this time he will make damn sure it is him. (*beat*) And looking back, he thinks they were right – to promote him when he was walking round the office bleary eyed after zero sleep and constantly on the phone to Jess would have been a risk. A high fucking risk! (*beat*) He sees that now. The game is competitive and there were better players then. But not now. Now he is ready. His domestic environment is under control, Jess is managing ok, Henry sleeps through the night... Henry!

TOGETHER: I miss him.

JESS: And she's taking out her mobile...

CHRIS: (*to Jess*) Watch out!

JESS: And they're looking at photos of Henry and the ache is so bad, she thinks (*to Chris*) I'm ready to go home now.

CHRIS: Yeah, I miss our little chap.

JESS: He might be walking.

CHRIS: I hope not. That would drive your mother mad. (*beat*) Jess, what will you do?

JESS: Do what when?

CHRIS: When we get back.

JESS: The same. Look after Henry. Clean the flat.

CHRIS: We could afford a cleaner.

JESS: It's four rooms.

CHRIS: Yeah, I... I thought you might want to go back to work?

JESS: I've got no work to go back to.

CHRIS: Alright, do something.

JESS: Looking after Henry is something.

CHRIS: Of course. (*beat*) He thinks about her friends at the wedding, bright and intelligent and animatedly talking about their Ph.D.s and... and he thinks about her and Henry, and he thinks where is the woman I wanted

	to marry? Where is the spark? He thinks she is living a half life.
JESS:	And she knows.
CHRIS:	(*speaking over her*) And he knows. (*beat*) He says nothing.
TOGETHER:	Because there are some things that it is ok to know but not to say.
JESS:	And she is fine.
CHRIS:	And he loves her. (*to Jess*) I meant do something for you. A hobby.
JESS:	I'm not your mother. What's the latest? Lap dancing.
CHRIS:	Kickboxing.
JESS:	(*laughs*) I don't need a hobby and we've got a babysitter now. We can see films and go for pizza.
CHRIS:	And that's enough?
JESS:	That's enough. (*pause*)
CHRIS:	Why don't you come off the anti-depressants?
JESS:	No.
CHRIS:	You're fine now, you…
JESS:	(*interrupts*) I said no.

10.

JESS: And she's still saying no and it's September 2009, a year on, and she is still taking the anti-depressants because why stop when you're onto something good? Why run the risk of not coping when you're coping? (*beat*) It's not that the pills stop her feeling, it's that they erase the hard edges so that she can feel, and life is ok again and she can function like everyone else and she doesn't mind about the things she can't do. (*beat*) She doesn't mind so much. And she knows that everyone can't do things. She means everyone has something they can't do.

CHRIS: (*talking over her*) But not everyone minds. (*beat*) And they are coasting, no not coasting, not exactly, he is working hard – keeping up, keeping in – but the banking crisis is rippling out across the city, the bubble has burst and there will be no more talk of junior partnerships, no more talk of expanding premises, instead muted whispers of downsizing, of restructuring exercises haunt the once confident water dispenser and in the news politicians with forced smiles speak an unfamiliar language, warning of austerity and double dip recession and he thinks what has happened to the world? (*beat*) Not that he is concerned personally of course – the firm's coffers are deep and he is a valued employee, a winner with an outstanding track record, (*beat*) but sometimes he looks at the faces of the newest interns, fresh faced out of law school, and he is happy not to be them.

(*pause*)

JESS: And one day he doesn't come home from work, and she thinks maybe he's gone to the pub but he doesn't do that very often because he wants to get home for Henry's bedtime.

CHRIS: They read stories.

JESS: And she's getting hungry and it's getting late and he'd promised to cook risotto with asparagus and camembert and now she's struggling to open a tin of beans. She's not good with tin openers but she's thinking that last time she managed it so why is it so bloody difficult now? And after several futile attempts, she manages to indent a small hole in the tin and cuts her finger, 'Ow!' and...

(*Chris enters, sees her bandaged finger*)

CHRIS: Are you alright?

JESS: Yes.

CHRIS: That looks...

JESS: (*interrupts*) Just a cut. It's nothing. (*beat*) Where have you been?

CHRIS: Can you let me get in the door first?

JESS: Are you drunk?

CHRIS: I'm pissed off.

JESS: What...?

CHRIS: Fucking pissed off.

JESS: SSHH!

CHRIS: I want to see him.

JESS: He's asleep.

CHRIS: I need to see him.

JESS: Well, come home before his bedtime.

CHRIS: Every night, I am home every night to…

JESS: (*interrupts*) I know.

CHRIS: One night, one night I stay out and you…

JESS: (*interrupts*) He missed you.

CHRIS: (*quietly*) Yeah.

JESS: And I didn't know what to say because I didn't know where you were. I texted you loads and phoned and…

CHRIS: My phone was on silent. (*beat*) I didn't want to look at it. (*beat*) I walked home.

JESS: Walked from where?

CHRIS: From the city.

JESS: From your work? Are you serious?

CHRIS: Fucking blisters on my right heel. (*beat*) And he wants to explain to her that it wasn't a rational decision, but that there he was, on the steps outside St Pauls, paralysed with anger and fear and wondering where was the nearest pub he could get pissed in without bumping into

	anyone from the office, and suddenly he was walking. (*beat*) He found himself walking. And walking and walking, and as he walked, he'd noticed how colourful everything was and how he felt he didn't want to get the tube because... (*beat, to Jess*) I've lost my job.
JESS:	What?
CHRIS:	(*to self*) And as he says it, the absurdity of the phrase makes him laugh. He hasn't lost his job, someone's taken it from him. He hasn't lost anything. His cases are in perfect order, he has never lost in court.
JESS:	You said it was safe.
CHRIS:	Because I believed it was. I thought those bastards appreciated me.
JESS:	Shit!
CHRIS:	Yeah.
JESS:	Fuck to them! After everything you've done...
CHRIS:	(*interrupts*) It's cheaper for them to employ someone more junior, it's that...
JESS:	(*interrupts*) That's so...

CHRIS: (*interrupts*) I'll find something else.

JESS: I hope so.

CHRIS: I am good at my job. Bloody good.

JESS: I just... I mean... it's tough out there now. That's what you keep saying, that...

CHRIS: (*interrupts*) I said I'll find something. (*beat*) If you look hard enough... I've always worked.

JESS: I had to look after Clive.

CHRIS: So...?

JESS: I... just... I mean

CHRIS: This is not about you, alright.

JESS: It affects all of us.

CHRIS: Don't make me feel bad! Don't start!

JESS: Maybe I could get a job.

CHRIS: You?

JESS: You're always saying I should do something...

CHRIS: (*interrupts*) And what job would you do?

JESS: I don't know exactly.

CHRIS: No. (*beat*) Do you know how much I earn? Do you know how much the mortgage costs?

JESS: I'm trying to help.

CHRIS: That is not helpful. That is seriously unhelpful.

JESS: I can do things.

CHRIS: (*looking away*) Yeah.

JESS: She looks at him.

CHRIS: (*talking over her*) He says nothing.

JESS: (*to Chris*) That's what you say. You say I can do things.

CHRIS: But not like other people. (*beat*) And he's said it and he didn't want to say it but he's said it and he can't unsay it.

JESS: What do you mean?

CHRIS: The things you can't do… they're… they're… I don't know.

JESS: What things?

CHRIS: You lose your keys.

JESS: So! You lose your keys.

CHRIS: Because I don't pay attention to not losing them. (*beat*) How about that wine the other night?

JESS: It's nearly all screw tops now and I just…

CHRIS: (*interrupts*) You were hysterical. A simple corkscrew and you're acting like the world's ended. (*beat*) And you can't open a tin or use scissors or a stapler, you can't iron, and you can't put the cover on the duvet.

JESS: You said you didn't mind.

CHRIS: That's not the point.

JESS: I'm rubbish with my hands, ok. Lots of people are rubbish with their hands.

CHRIS: It matters to you.

JESS: Of course it matters. (*beat*) Is this about Henry?

CHRIS: No.

JESS: Do you think I can't look after him?

CHRIS: No! You're brilliant at looking after him. (*beat*) At the bits that matter.

JESS: And what bits don't matter?

CHRIS: I don't know. Putting his shoes on, dressing him, cutting his fringe…

JESS: (*interrupts*) I'm not a hairdresser.

CHRIS: (*speaking over her*) …Cooking his meals without a…

JESS: (*interrupts*) You said... you said in a relationship one person is good at some things and one person is good at other things and that's ok.

CHRIS: It's ok for me.

JESS: Well, it doesn't sound like it.

CHRIS: Alright, it's... frustrating, sometimes.

JESS: And you piss me off too.

CHRIS: Jess, come on, I'm not... look, things are not ok for *you*, that's my point. (*beat*) I think you should see a doctor.

JESS: What?

CHRIS: Get some medical advice about all this.

JESS: What do you think I have a medical condition? (*beat*) I'm not ill. Or is this about the anti-depressants again?

CHRIS: No, but there's another thing. (*slowly*) Why do you still need those bloody pills? You keep saying you're happy.

(*pause*)

JESS: Some people are prone to depression, ok. I can't help it. And if I need to take a pill every day, so what?

CHRIS: I don't buy it. That's what. I don't buy it.

JESS: Why are you getting at me like this? Is it my fault you've lost your job?

CHRIS: And he wants to explain to her that when your world shifts unexpectedly, there is a space where you can say things you've never said before because you didn't know you needed to say them. (*to Jess*) See a doctor.

JESS: Fuck off!

11.

JESS: And her GP listens, when she visits him four weeks later. He is a good listener, and he listens attentively and asks her all sorts of questions, and says it's rubbish. Of course she's normal and to tell the truth, he's not very practically minded either, but he wonders whether she'd like her anti-depressants upped or put her name down for six weeks of CBT? And she says no to both, she's fine with her current levels of medication and therapy's not her thing and he goes quiet and sighs and says, 'With your husband out of work, more support would be beneficial'. And she says no, again, 'I'm fine.' And he pauses and suggests that perhaps she could take up something to occupy her mind, to stop her worrying about inconsequential matters. And she says, 'Losing my keys every day is not inconsequential.' And he laughs, he thinks it's a joke and he says, 'Well, no.' And she says, 'I'd like to have a job.' And he says, 'That's an excellent idea, as long as you get the balance right.' (*beat*) And she thinks when has she ever got the balance right for anything ever? (*pause*) And walking back form the doctors' along the Portobello Road to collect Henry from preschool, she feels liberated, she is normal. This is the official medical opinion – she is normal and she's skipping in the street and everything's fine – only it's not really because inside, somewhere inside, she is disappointed because... because the GP... he doesn't know her. (*beat*) Chris knows her. (*beat*) And later she tells him. (*to Chris*) The GP says I'm absolutely fine.

CHRIS: (*not looking at her, drinking*) Yeah.
JESS: He's not talking much.
CHRIS: He's busy.
JESS: He's drinking.
CHRIS: It's under control.

(*pause*)

JESS: And so she gets a job.

CHRIS: He is looking.

JESS: Walking past a bookshop in Westbourne Grove with Henry one day, 'Look where you're going!' she stops to wipe his nose, 'You are so full of cold!' and sees an advert in the window.

CHRIS: Every day he is looking.

JESS: And every morning, she drops Henry off, and walks to the bookshop and starts work.

CHRIS: This website, that website. Emails to his mates, 'Know of anything going?'

JESS: She feels she is doing something.

CHRIS: (*to Jess*) They pay you a pittance.

JESS: (*to Chris*) It's something.

CHRIS: He is looking.

JESS: There are things she can't do – opening and shutting the windows and changing the till roll but everywhere there are things she can't do and that's ok and there are things she can do – talking to the customers and selling books. She's friendly and helpful and really very good at it. (*to Chris*) I like it.

CHRIS: It's hardly a vocation.

JESS: And he's drinking more and more.

CHRIS: (*to Jess*) I'm alright.

JESS: And at night he's asleep on the sofa.

CHRIS: (*yawning*) Too tired to move.

JESS: And she's glad not to have the stink of alcohol in her, in their, room but sad and... (*beat*) And they start by not sharing the small things.

CHRIS: He's got knocked back from another interview.

JESS: Henry had his face painted at preschool.

CHRIS: His mum's got another new boyfriend.

JESS: But he fell off the scooter and has a real shiner.

(*pause*)

CHRIS: And then they are not sharing the big things.

JESS: Which school should she put Henry's name down for?

CHRIS: Some days he feels like giving up on the city.
TOGETHER: They are in different spaces.
JESS: But there is Henry.
TOGETHER: They love their son.

12.

CHRIS: It is September 2011, Henry looks smart in his school uniform...

JESS: Adorable!

CHRIS: ...And he has a job. A property firm in South London. It is shit pay with shit prospects and not in the city which is shit and his bosses are uninspiring but it is a job and in this climate you're lucky to have anything. (*beat*) And he has a wife and son to provide for. He has responsibilities (*beat*) and he has stopped the booze. (*beat*) No, not stopped, he enjoys a beer after work or a bottle of Chardonnay at the weekend...

JESS: (*clinks glass*) They do things together again.

CHRIS: ...He has stopped drinking unhealthily.

JESS: And they talk to one another.

CHRIS: They talk about the day to day stuff.

JESS: Henry, and the bookshop, and his work, and what he's going to cook for their tea.

CHRIS: And is Henry old enough for a long haul flight?

JESS: Definitely not!

CHRIS: Too much of a livewire.

JESS: And in the bookshop she's happy!

CHRIS: (*to Jess*) Are you?

JESS: I'm fine.

CHRIS: Everything is fine but he is biding his time because markets are cyclical and things will change and he is sharp and he will get back on course. (*beat*) He doesn't talk about it to her.

JESS: They don't talk about everything.

CHRIS: But he wants the moon. (*beat*) He is hungry again.

(*pause*)

JESS: And one day Henry's teacher calls her in and says that she's observed from Henry's behaviour and learning profile that he could have a recognisable condition, an ASD, and a diagnosis would benefit him and would she agree to this?

CHRIS: A what?

JESS: Autistic Spectrum Disorder.

CHRIS: My son is not autistic.

JESS: No, well it could be all sorts of things.

CHRIS: What things?

JESS: Dyslexia, dyspraxia, dyscalculia, Aspergers Syndrome, ADHD, ADD, OCD, Tourettes.

CHRIS: Sounds like some textbook bollocks to me.

JESS: It's all here in the leaflet. If you have a read...

CHRIS: I've got an application to finish.

JESS: It'll only take a minute.

CHRIS: The deadline's tonight.

JESS: This is important.

CHRIS: Giving our son some kind of label?

JESS: You know he still can't ride his bike...

CHRIS: (*interrupts*) Alright, I'll take him to the park on Sunday.

JESS: Well, this could be why. He can't coordinate...

CHRIS: (*interrupts*) Look, he needs more practice, alright. (*beat*) It's that simple.

JESS: And you keep saying he's clumsy, like there's something wrong with him.

CHRIS: I don't keep saying it.

JESS: Last night.

CHRIS: I'd just finished ironing that shirt and your tea was scalding.

JESS: At least it was just your shirt.

CHRIS: It was a bloody expensive one!

JESS: He could have burnt himself.

CHRIS: So don't put hot drinks on the table.

JESS: I put it down for a second, ok. You know what he's like. (*beat*) I'm sorry. (*beat*) Can I fill out the forms? For the appointment?

CHRIS: It looks like you've already done it. (*beat*) And he wants to tell her that he loves his son for who he is and that's all and that's everything.

JESS: You need to sign. (*beat*) And she wants to tell him that there's something about Henry that... she can't quite articulate what she means... but something... something she doesn't want to hide.

CHRIS: (*sighs*) Henry's fine.

JESS: I know but... I think this will help him.

CHRIS: If his teacher suggested it.

JESS: (*beat*) Will you come to the appointment?

CHRIS: It's difficult to take time off work.

JESS: I'd like you to come.

13.

CHRIS: Three months later, December 2011, he takes an afternoon off.

JESS: They both do.

CHRIS: Because it is his son and it is the right thing to do. And his work said yes, but if they'd have said no, he would have insisted. (*beat*) It's not that he has any gravitas at the firm, not seriously, it's that he doesn't care. (*beat*) No, no he cares – he is conscientious and efficient and he wins cases – he doesn't care as much, (*beat*) not like before. (*beat*) This is a mediocre firm, it pays the bills and he keeps his hand in – he doesn't give a shit. (*beat*) He's waiting for something better.

JESS: And on the way home in the cab, after Henry's been dropped back at school, (*to Henry*) 'Have a good day, darling'

CHRIS: (*to Henry*) I'll see you later.

JESS: ...they sit apart, looking out of the window at the Christmas trees and the lights in the shop windows.

CHRIS: They don't look at each other.

JESS: Not like they used to.

CHRIS: They are completely overwhelmed.

JESS: They've known it all along.

CHRIS: (*to Jess*) We didn't have a name for it before.

JESS: No, but it all makes such sense.

CHRIS: Who makes up these names?

JESS: I don't know.

CHRIS: Honestly, it doesn't exactly trip off the tongue.

JESS: They used to call it 'clumsy child syndrome'.

CHRIS: Yeah, I think I prefer that.

JESS: No, it's insulting.

CHRIS: At least it says what it is.

JESS: Well, it refers to one aspect of the condition in a negative way.

CHRIS: What's so bad about clumsy?

JESS: Nothing, but... it's not... oh nothing. (*beat*) I think the name's ok and, you know, law is full of Latinate terms. You used to show off with them.

CHRIS: Did I?

JESS:	When I first met you. All of the time.
CHRIS:	(*beat*) I'm bored of law.
JESS:	Really?
CHRIS:	(*quickly*) I'm bored of work. (*to self*) That's what he tells her, he's bored of work, and it is true, but something has hit him in the dark like a punch in his stomach because... because... he can't explain it. (*beat*) Because a successful career in the law is his dream, junior partnership, senior partnership, a practice in his name, this is his dream, has always been, and if he is bored of law...
JESS:	(*interrupts*) Me too. I'm constantly clockwatching.
CHRIS:	Yeah? I thought you loved that bloody place?
JESS:	It's safe. I like that it's safe.
CHRIS:	I wouldn't be so sure about that.
JESS:	What?
CHRIS:	That staircase is a health and safety no no.
JESS:	My life is a health and safety no no.
CHRIS:	Yup, I'd go with that.

JESS: Wrong answer!

CHRIS: True answer!

JESS: And suddenly…

CHRIS: (*speaking over her*) Suddenly they are laughing.

JESS: Together.

CHRIS: They haven't laughed for a long time.

JESS: Not together. (*pause*) Their son has a diagnosis of developmental dyspraxia, an autistic spectrum disorder, affecting co-ordination…

CHRIS: Gross and fine motor skills,

JESS: And working memory,

CHRIS: Concentration and organisation,

TOGETHER: And they are laughing.

(*pause*)

JESS: Did you learn Latin at your posh school?

CHRIS: I sat in the classroom. I don't know if I learned anything.

JESS: So translate it for me – (*pronounces slowly*) dys-prax-ia.

CHRIS: (*groaning*) It's not rocket science, Jess. Not practical, without practical skills.

JESS: Well, that's certainly Henry.

CHRIS: That's him. (*pause. They look at one another*) He sees her.

JESS: She lets him see her. (*they touch hands. Pause*)

CHRIS: Thanks for sorting it out.

JESS: It was Mrs Brook's suggestion. I didn't do anything.

CHRIS: I would have thrown the forms in the bin. (*beat*) Jesus!

JESS: Thanks for coming.

CHRIS: Thank God, I did! (*beat*) I'm on it now.

JESS: On what?

CHRIS: On making sure he gets what he needs. As soon as the educational psychologist's report comes in, we'll get cracking on the recommendations.

JESS: I'm sure the school will be helpful.

CHRIS: It's not only the classroom learning assistant, we'll need to sort the out of school

	support. Occupational therapy, speech and language, cognitive…
JESS:	Stop!
CHRIS:	Jess?
JESS:	Just a minute. Slow down. We need to, you know, take things slowly.
CHRIS:	He has a condition and I want him to get the best support.
JESS:	I just mean not everything at once.
CHRIS:	Come on, you're the one who set this up and I am taking it seriously.
JESS:	I know.
CHRIS:	And I don't mind paying. (*beat*) We could put him into private school that…
JESS:	(*interrupts*) He's happy at school.
CHRIS:	I suppose.
JESS:	Let's see how he gets on with the school support first. We don't want to overwhelm him.
CHRIS:	Alright, alright.

14.

JESS: (*at computer*) It's later that evening, December 2011, and her son has developmental dyspraxia and researching his condition on the web, she finds herself clicking on the adult section and... and she... and she thinks... she thinks this could be me. (*beat*) No... this is me. (*beat*) This is who I am.

CHRIS: He comes into the room and he looks at her.

JESS: (*speaking over him*) She looks at him.

CHRIS: (*reading over her shoulder*) He thinks how can you know something and not know it at the same time? How can a life, his life, be lived like that?

JESS: She says, 'If I'd have known.'

CHRIS: He says, 'If we'd have known.' He says, 'You've got a name for it now.' He thinks she looks the same, how she's always looked but something is different. (*beat*) He can't describe it, there are no discernible features, but something has changed in her. In her,

	and in him, and between them and… it is good.
JESS:	She says, 'Before it was like a jigsaw. You've got all the pieces there in front of you but you can't put them together.'
CHRIS:	He says, 'I hate jigsaws.'
JESS:	She says, 'It's a disability.'
CHRIS:	He says, reading the screen, 'It's an alternability.'
JESS:	She says, 'Fuck you!', and they are laughing and… and she says, 'I'll give up my job now.'
CHRIS:	Yeah?
JESS:	Yeah.
CHRIS:	And what will you do?
JESS:	Think. (*beat*) I've got a lot to think about.
CHRIS:	You could go back to the Ph.D.?
JESS:	No. (*beat*)
CHRIS:	I'm sure you'd get support, if you did decide…
JESS:	No. (*beat*) And she wants to explain to him that she's been hiding, (*beat*) all of her life, until this point now, here in the room with

him, she's been hiding, (*beat*) and she wants to explain that she doesn't want to hide now. (*beat*) She wants to explain that you can't exist if you don't have a name and if you can't exist, you have to hide away. (*beat*) She wants to explain all of this, but she can't say anything.

(*Jess tries to talk but can't*)

CHRIS: He gets it.
JESS: (*speaking over him*) He gets it.
CHRIS: So…? What are you going to do?
JESS: Number One…
CHRIS: Not another list, Jess!
JESS: (*talking over him*) Number One: make sure Henry's ok and Number Two: think about what I want to do.
CHRIS: That sounds like a plan.
JESS: I like planning.
CHRIS: And you are bloody brilliant at it.
JESS: Thank you. (*pause*) And how about your job?

CHRIS: My job! (*beat*) He thinks that's all it is a job. Something to do to pay the bills. Gainful employment. (*beat*) He thinks about getting back on course. (*beat*) He thinks it is possible he will never have the moon. (*beat*) He looks at her.

JESS: (*speaking over him*) She looks at him.

CHRIS: And that in this moment, that is quite alright.

END.